Super Safari 1

Letters and Numbers Workbook

CAMBRIDGE
UNIVERSITY PRESS

Color in Polly!

CAMBRIDGE
UNIVERSITY PRESS

University Printing House, Cambridge CB2 8BS, United Kingdom

One Liberty Plaza, 20th Floor, New York, NY 10006, USA

477 Williamstown Road, Port Melbourne, VIC 3207, Australia

314–321, 3rd Floor, Plot 3, Splendor Forum, Jasola District Centre, New Delhi – 110025, India

79 Anson Road, #06–04/06, Singapore 079906

Torre de los Parques, Colonia Tlacoquemécatl del Valle, Mexico City cp 03200, Mexico

Cambridge University Press is part of the University of Cambridge.

It furthers the University's mission by disseminating knowledge in the pursuit of education, learning and research at the highest international levels of excellence.

www.cambridge.org
Information on this title: www.cambridge.org/978-1-316-60949-1

First published 2016

20 19 18 17 16 15 14 13 12 11 10 9 8 7

Printed in Malaysia by Vivar Printing

A catalogue record for this publication is available from the British Library

ISBN 978-1-316-60949-1 Letters and Numbers Workbook 1

Additional resources for this publication at www.cambridge.org/supersafari

Cambridge University Press has no responsibility for the persistence or accuracy of URLs for external or third-party internet websites referred to in this publication, and does not guarantee that any content on such websites is, or will remain, accurate or appropriate. Information regarding prices, travel timetables, and other factual information given in this work is correct at the time of first printing but Cambridge University Press does not guarantee the accuracy of such information thereafter.

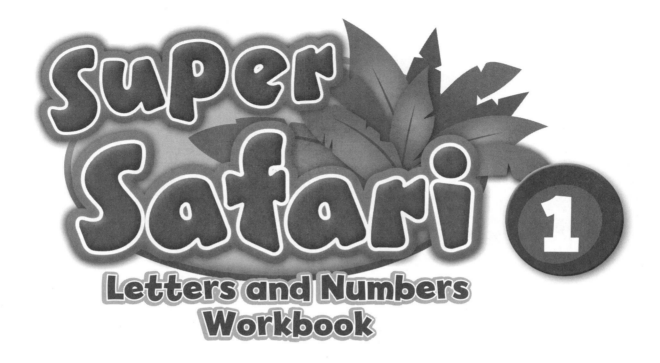

Super Safari 1

Letters and Numbers Workbook

Hello!

The children trace the circle with their index finger. Then they trace the circle with different colored crayons several times. Finally, the children color the picture freely.

1 **Trace and color.**

Hello! I'm Polly.

1 Color the pictures.

The children point to the girl in the picture and say *hello* aloud. Repeat the procedure with the boy. Finally, the children color the picture freely.

1 My class

The children trace the lines with their index finger first, and then with different colored crayons several times. Then they identify the objects. Finally, the children color the pictures freely.

1 Trace and color.

1 **Count and trace. Color the objects.**

The children identify the objects and count them aloud.
Then they trace the number with their index finger first, and then with different colored crayons several times. Finally, the children color the objects freely.

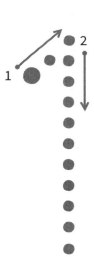

1 Trace and color.

The children trace the lines with their index finger first, and with different colored crayons several times. Say *Boy, hands up. Boy, hands down*. The children point to the corresponding pictures. Repeat with the other rows. Finally, the children color the pictures freely.

1 **Count and trace. Color the pictures.**

The children count the boys aloud. Then the children trace the number with their index finger first, and then with different colored crayons several times. Finally, they color in the picture freely.

1 **Trace and color.**

The children trace the lines with their index finger first, and then with different colored crayons. The children identify the books, the boy, the girl and the school. The children point to the pictures. Finally, the children color the pictures freely.

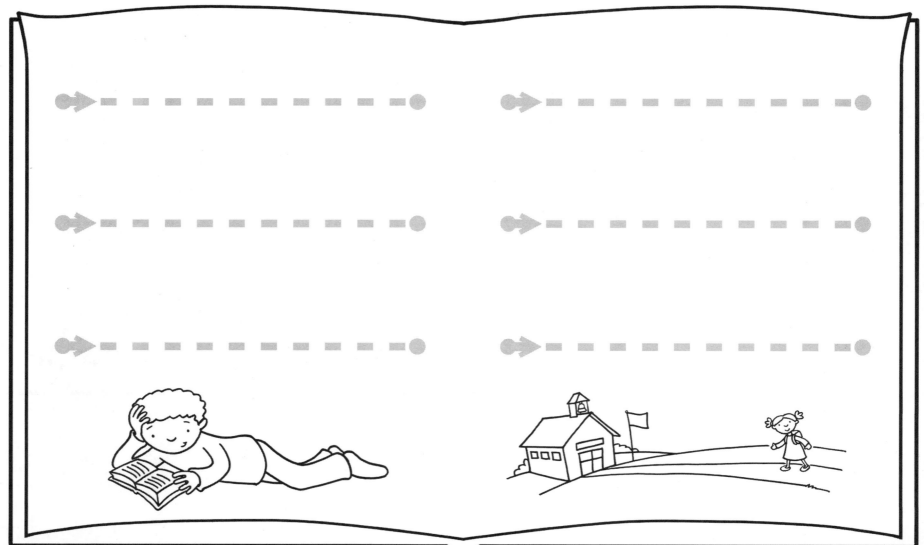

1 **Count and color. Trace the numbers.**

The children point to the characters and count them aloud. Then the children color them. Finally, they trace the numbers with different colored crayons several times.

1 **Trace and color.**

The children say /p/ – /p/ – /p/ – *pencil*. Then they trace the letter and color in the picture freely. Finally, the children color the pictures that start with letter /p/.

1 Color and cut. Assemble the booklet.

Color and cut. Assemble the booklet.

Materials:

scissors, crayons

Instructions:

The children name the items. Then they color in the objects. Help children cut out the booklet. Finally, help the children fold the pages to make the booklet.

1 **Match and color.**

2 My colors

The children trace the lines with their index finger and with different colored crayons several times. Then the children identify the objects and color them freely.

1 Trace and color.

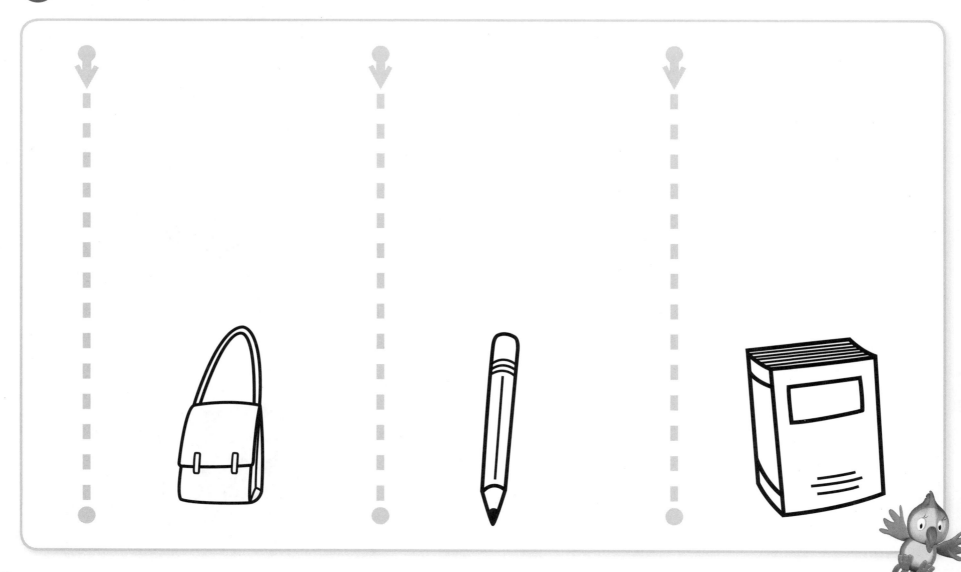

1 **Count and trace. Color the objects.**

The children count the cans aloud. Then they trace the number with their index finger first, and then with different colored crayons several times. Finally, the children color the cans of paint according to the instructions: *Point to the can. Color the can red.*

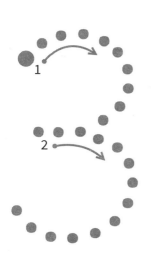

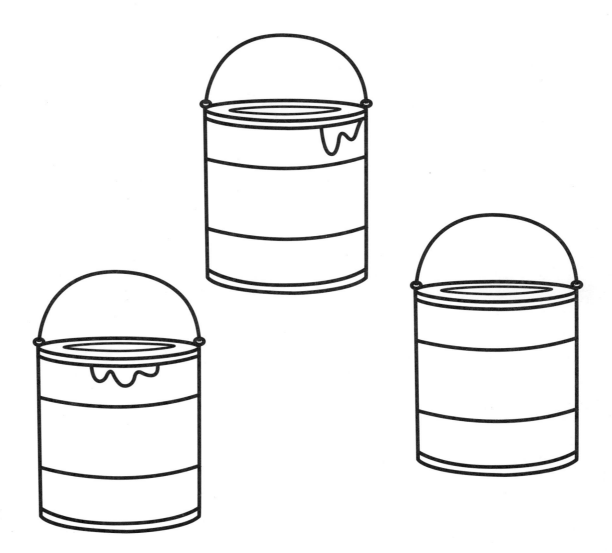

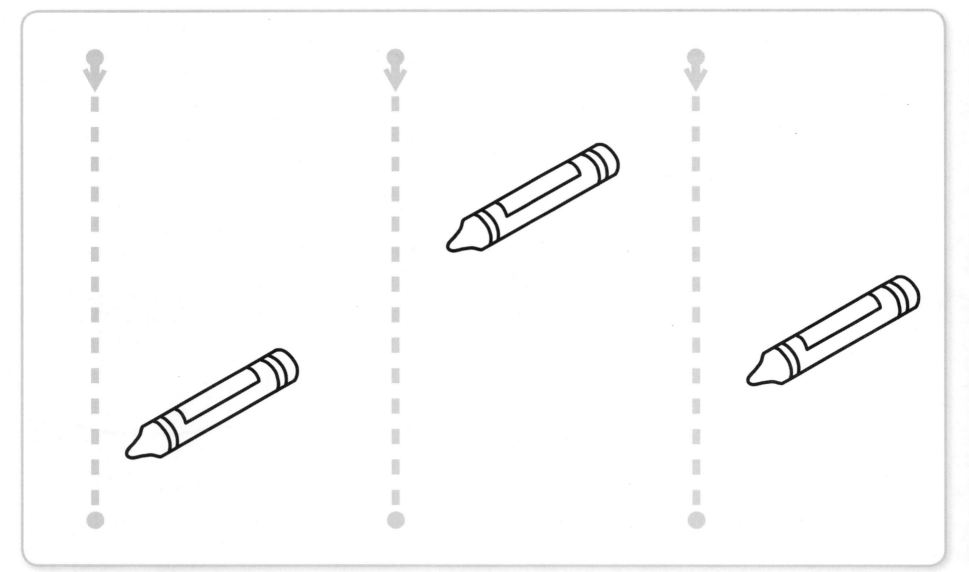

1 Count and trace. Color the objects.

The children count the books aloud. Then the children trace the number with their index finger first, and then with different colored crayons several times. Finally, the children color the pictures freely.

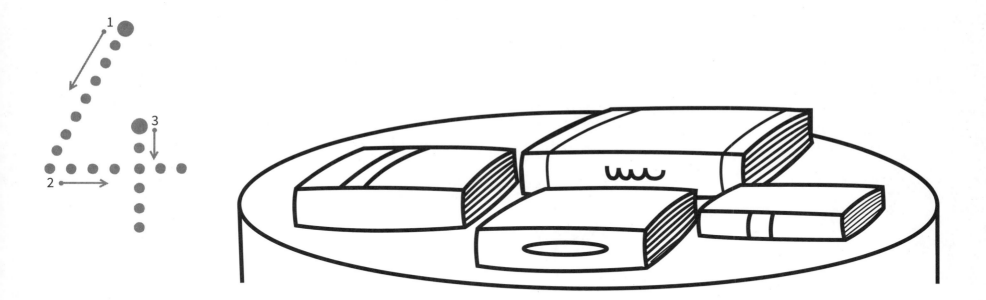

1 Trace and color.

The children trace the lines with different colored crayons. Finally, the children name and color the characters freely.

1 **Count and trace. Color the pictures.**

The children count the girls aloud. Then they trace the numbers with different colored crayons several times. Finally, they color the pictures freely.

1 **Trace and color.**

The children say /b/ – /b/ – /b/ – *bag*. Then they trace the letter and color in the picture freely. Finally, the children color the pictures that start with the letter /b/.

1 Color and glue.

Color and glue.

Materials:
scissors, colored tissue paper (red, blue, green, yellow), glue, colored markers

Preparation:
Cut small squares of colored tissue paper.

Instructions:
The children use a blue marker to color in the first section in the rainbow. Then distribute glue and the blue tissue paper. Help the children spread the glue on the blue section. Show the children how to glue the blue tissue paper on the corresponding section. Continue in the same manner with the green and yellow sections of the rainbow.

1 Trace and color the objects.

The children trace the objects. Then they color in the objects freely.

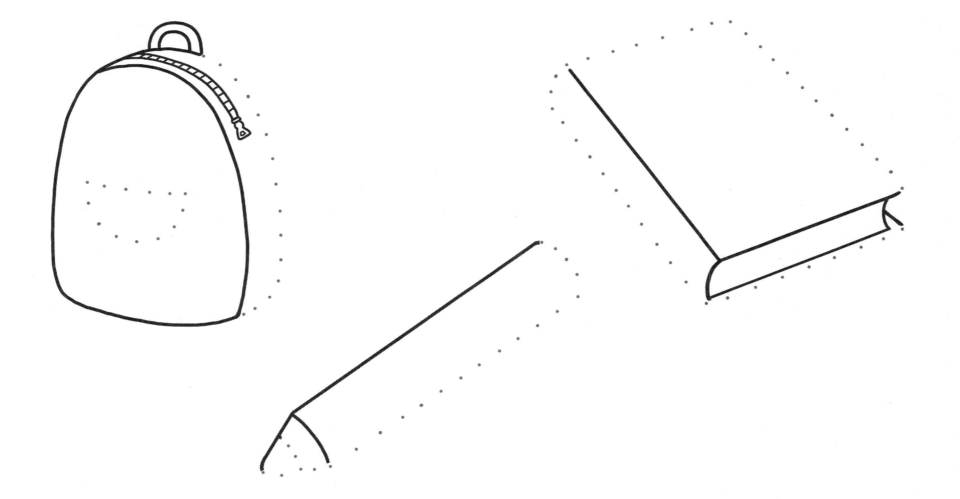

3 My family

The children trace the circle with their index finger first, and then with different colored crayons several times. Finally, the children identify the family members and color the picture freely.

1 Trace and color.

1 **Count and trace. Color the pictures.**

The children identify the family members and count them aloud. Then they trace the numbers with different colored crayons several times. Finally, the children color the pictures freely.

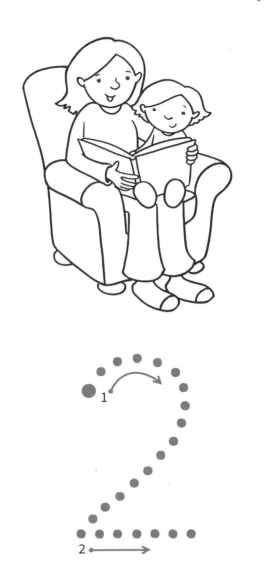

1 Trace and color.

The children trace the circles with different colored crayons several times. Finally, the children identify the family member and color the picture freely.

1 **Count and match.**

1 2 3 4

1 **Trace and color.**

The children trace the circles with different colored crayons several times. Finally, the children identify the family members and color the pictures freely.

1 Trace and count. Color the pictures.

The children identify and trace the numbers. Then they identify the family members. Finally, they color the corresponding number of people.

1 Trace and color.

The children say /d/ – /d/ – /d/ – *dad*. Then they trace the letter and color in the picture freely. Finally, the children color the pictures that start with the letter /d/.

1 Color and assemble the puzzle.

Color and assemble the puzzle.

Materials:
crayons, scissors, glue, paper (1 sheet per student)

Instructions:
The children identify the family members.
Then the children color the picture.
Help them cut out the puzzle pieces.
The children assemble the puzzle and
glue it onto a sheet of paper.

1 **Draw your family.**

The children draw their families inside the picture frame.
Finally, they describe their families to the rest of the class.

This is my family.

4 My toys

The children trace the lines with their index fingers first, and then with different colored crayons. Finally, the children identify the toys and color them in freely.

1 Trace and color.

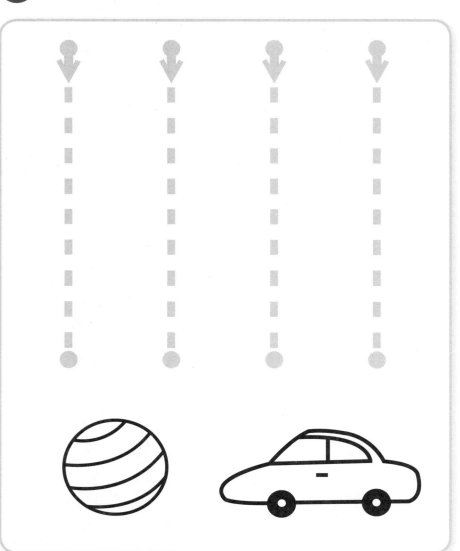

1 **Count and trace. Color the picture.**

The children count the balls aloud. Then the children trace the number with their index finger first, and then with different colored crayons several times. Finally, the children color the picture.

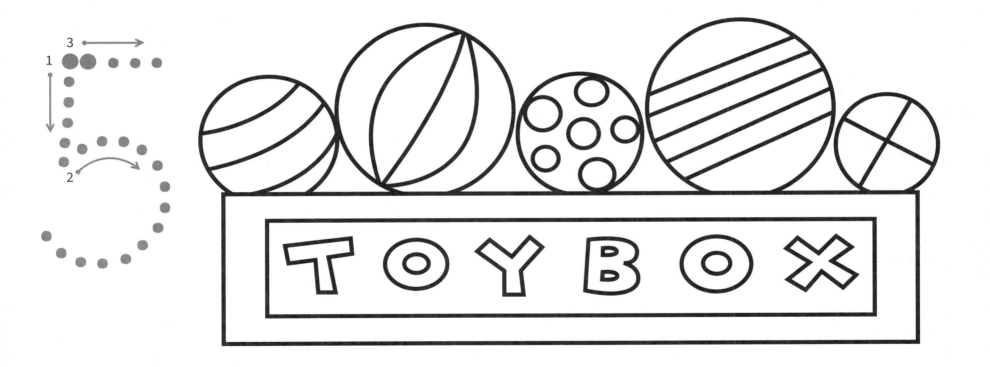

1 Trace and say.

The children trace the lines with their index finger first, and then with different colored crayons. Finally, the children say the patterns: *big ball, small ball, big ball, small ball; big doll, small doll...*

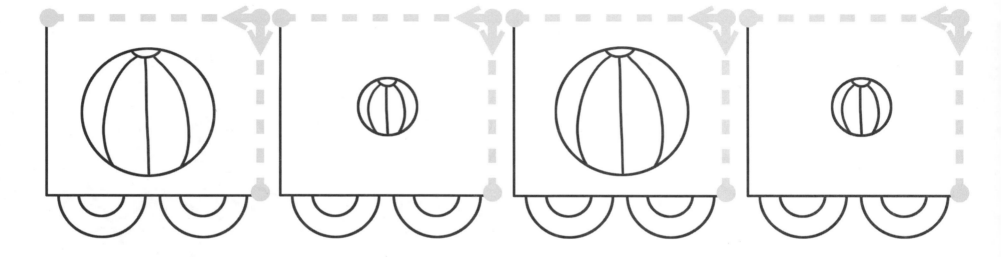

1 **Count and trace. Color the picture.**

The children count the dolls aloud. Then the children trace the number with their index finger first, and then with different colored crayons several times. Finally, the children color the picture freely.

1 Trace and color.

The children trace all the lines with different colored crayons. Then the children name the character and the toys. Finally, the children color in the picture.

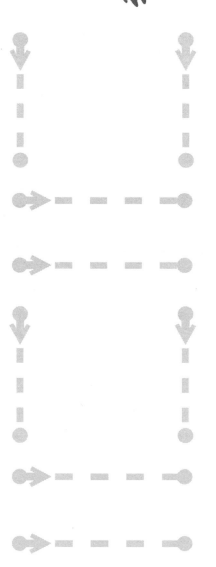

1 **Count and color.**

The children identify the numbers. Then they count the toys aloud. Finally, the children color the pictures freely.

1 2 3 4 5 6

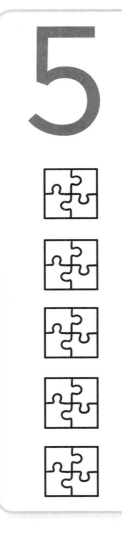

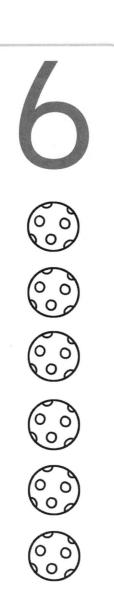

1 **Trace and color.**

The children say /c/ – /c/ – /c/ – *car*. Then the children trace the letter and color in the picture freely. Finally, the children color the pictures that start with the letter /c/.

1 Color and cut. Play a game.

Color and cut. Play a game.

Materials:
crayons, scissors

Preparation:
Help the children cut out the cards.

Instructions:
The children color the cards. Help them cut the cards out.
Demonstrate how the *Memory game* is played.
Divide the class into pairs. The children use only one set of cards. They shuffle the cards and place them face down on the table. Then each child takes a turn turning over two cards and finding matching pairs. The child with the most number of pair of cards wins.

1 Cut and glue.

The children color in the toy box with colored crayons. Then the children look for pictures of toys in old magazines. Help the children cut out the pictures. Finally, the children glue the pictures inside the toy box.

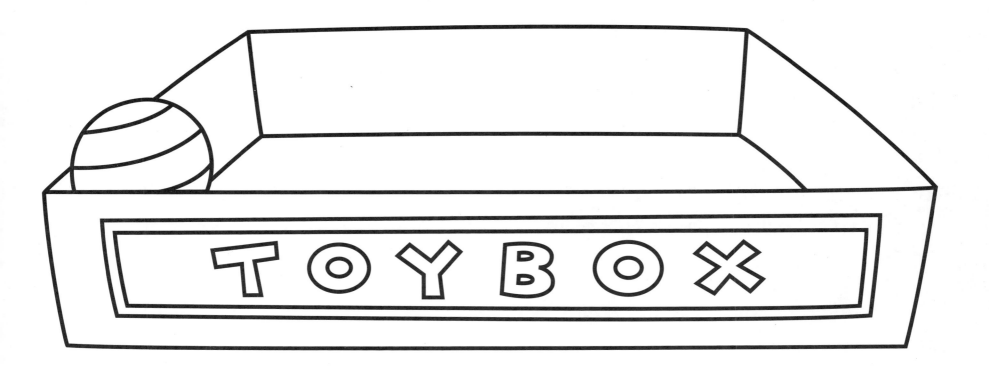

5 My numbers

1 Trace and color.

1 Trace and draw.

The children identify and trace the numbers with different colors. Then they draw the corresponding number of objects, e.g. *one book*, *two crayons*, *three balls*.

1 1 1

2 2 2

3 3 3

1 **Trace and color.**

The children trace the circles with their index finger first, and then they trace them with different colored crayons. Finally, the children color the picture freely.

1 **Trace. Count and color.**

The children say the numbers aloud. Then they trace the numbers with different colored crayons. Finally, the children count and color the corresponding number of items.

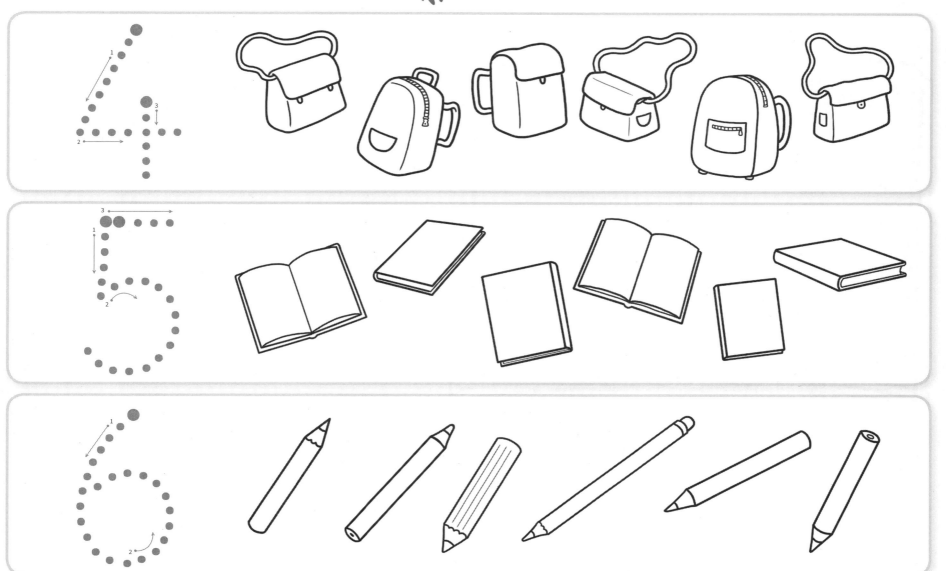

1 Trace and say.

The children trace the circles with their index finger first, and then they trace the circles with different colored crayons. Finally, the children identify the items.

1 **Count and match.**

The children identify the numbers. Then they count and match the numbers with the corresponding items. Finally, they color the items freely.

1   2   3   4   5

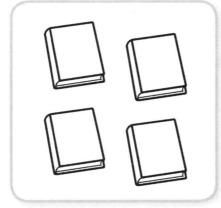

1 **Trace and color.**

The children say /t/ – /t/ – /t/ – *teddy*. Then the children trace the letter and color in the picture freely. Finally, the children color the pictures that start with letter /t/.

1 Cut and assemble. Spin and say.

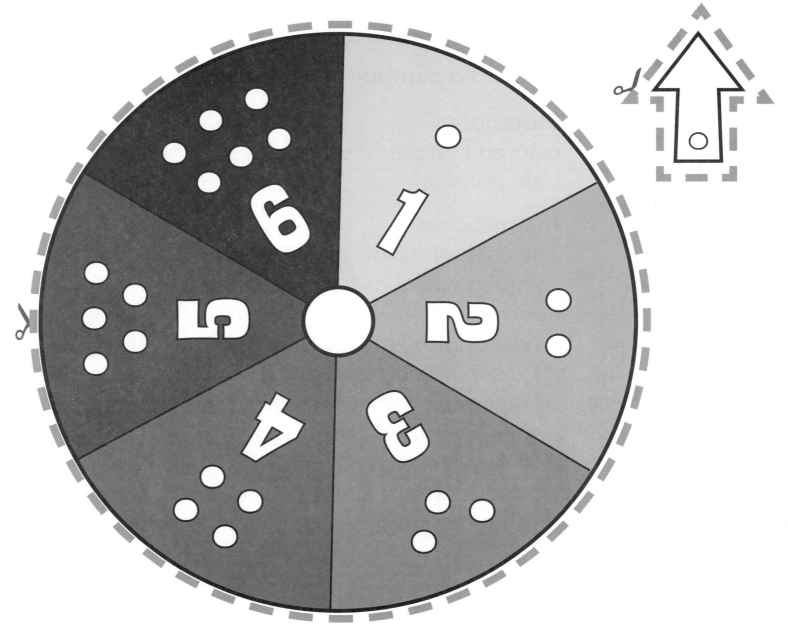

Cut and assemble. Spin and say.

Materials:
colored crayons, scissors, paper fastener, hole punch

Instructions:
The children color and cut out the spinning wheel and the arrow. Punch a hole through the spinning wheel and the arrow. Help the children attach the arrow to the spinning wheel with the paper fastener. Finally, invite different children to spin their wheel, count the number of dots and say the number out loud.

1 Draw and count.

The children draw one more toy in each box. The children count aloud the total number of toys in each toy box. Finally, the children color in the pictures freely.

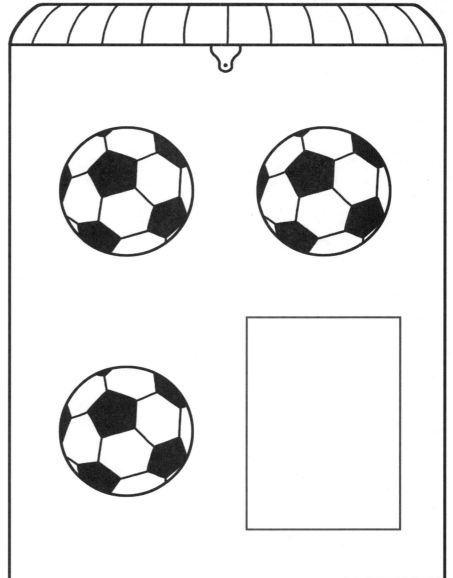

6 My pets

The children trace the spiral with their index finger first, and then they trace it with different colored crayons three times. Finally, the children identify the pet and color the picture freely.

1 Trace and color.

1 Trace and count. Color the picture.

The children trace the number with their index finger first, and then with different colored crayons several times. Finally, they count the cats aloud and color the picture freely.

1 Trace and color.

The children trace the spirals with different colored crayons. Then they identify the pets and name them aloud. Finally, they color in the picture freely.

1 **Count and trace. Color the picture.**

The children count the birds aloud. Then they trace the number with their index finger first, and then with different colored crayons several times. Finally, the children color in the picture freely.

The children trace the spirals with different colored crayons. Then they identify the actions and the pets. Finally, the children color the pets freely.

1 **Count and circle.**

The children count the pets aloud. Then the children circle the corresponding numbers. Finally, the children color the pets freely.

7 / 8

7 / 8

1 **Trace and color.**

The children say /e/ – /e/ – /e/ – *egg*. Then they trace the letter and color in the picture freely. Finally, the children color the pictures that start with letter /e/.

1 Cut and assemble.

Cut and assemble.

Materials:
cardboard paper, scissors, crayons, glue stick

Instructions:
The children color in the bird and the clouds. Then help the children cut out the pictures. Next, help them glue the bird and the clouds onto construction paper and cut them out again. Show the children how to assemble the bird to make it stand.

1 Match and color.

The children point to the pets *Point to the small bunny. Point to the big bunny.* The children match the big pets to the small pets. Finally, the children color the pets.

7 My food

The children trace the "s" shape with their index finger first, and then with different colored crayons several times. Finally, the children identify the food and color the pictures freely.

1 Trace and color.

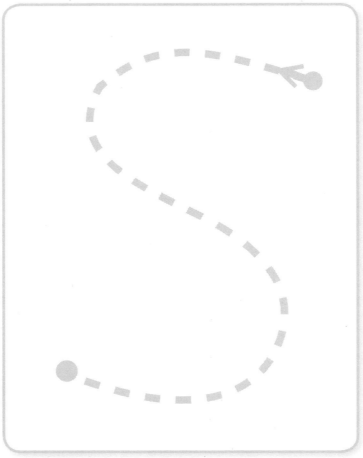

1 Count and trace.

The children count the scoops of ice cream aloud. Then the children trace the numbers with different colored crayons. Finally, they color in the pictures freely.

1 **Trace and color.**

The children trace the "s" shape with their index finger first, and then with different colored crayons several times. Finally, the children identify the food and color the pictures freely.

1 **Count and circle. Color the pictures.**

The children count the vegetables aloud, and then they circle the corresponding number. Finally, the children color the pictures freely.

5/6

7/8

1 Trace and say. Color the pictures.

The children trace the "s" shapes with different colored crayons. The children identify the food and say whether they like it or not, *Laura, what is this? Spaghetti. I like spaghetti.* Finally, the children color the food freely.

1 Count and match. Trace the numbers.

The children count the number of slices in each cake aloud.
Then they match the cakes with the corresponding numbers.
Finally, the children trace the numbers.

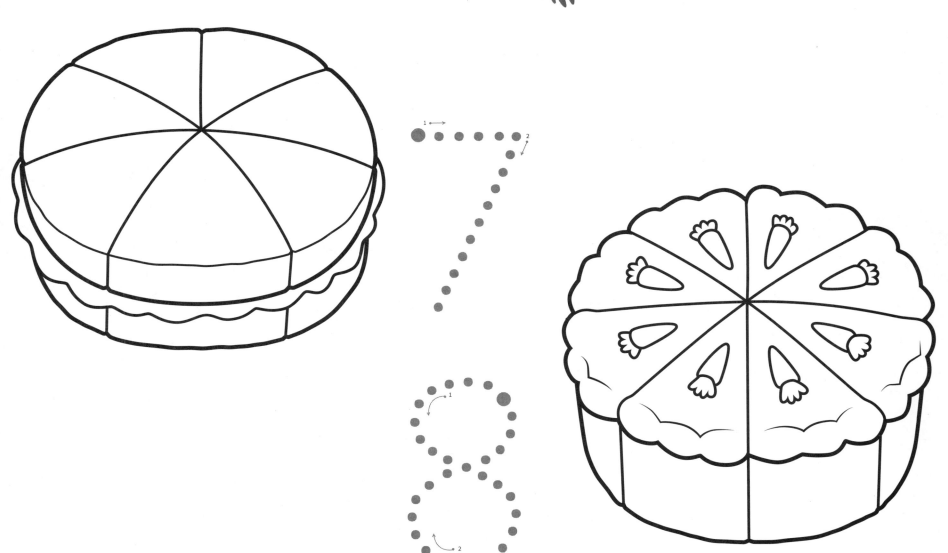

1 **Trace and color.**

The children say /s/ – /s/ – /s/ – *salad*. Then they trace the letter and color in the picture freely. Finally, the children color the pictures that start with letter /s/.

1 **Cut and glue.**

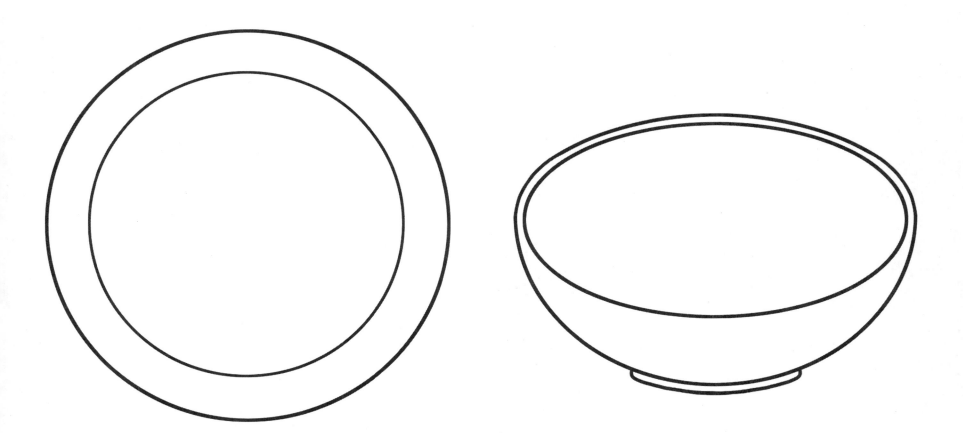

Cut and glue.

Materials:
colored markers, yellow yarn, rice,
glue, scissors

Preparation:
Cut the yarn into 10 cm lengths.

Instructions:
The children color in the plate and the bowl
with the markers. Then they glue
the yellow yarn onto the plate as
spaghetti. Next, the children spread
glue inside the bowl and sprinkle on
some rice. Finally, the children say
if they like the food or not.

1 **Match and say. Color the pictures.**

The children point to the food. Then they match the food they like to the happy face. Next, the children say *I like...* Finally, the children color in the pictures.

8 My clothes

The children trace the lines with their index finger first, and then with different colored crayons several times. Finally, the children identify each of the clothing items and color the pictures freely.

1 Trace and color.

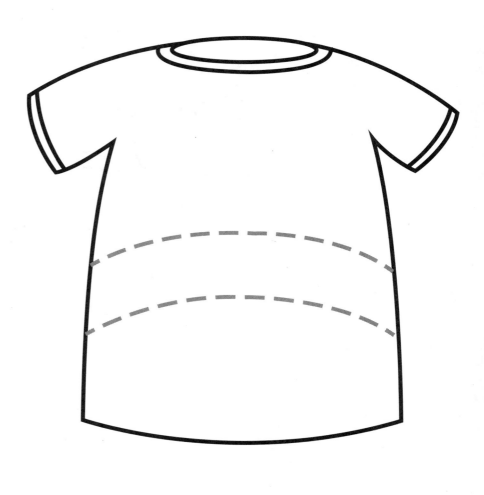

1 Count and trace. Color the picture.

The children count the T-shirts aloud. Then the children trace the number with their index fingers first, and then with different colored crayons several times. Finally, the children color in the pictures.

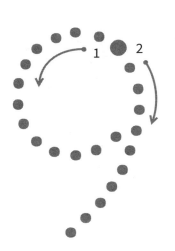

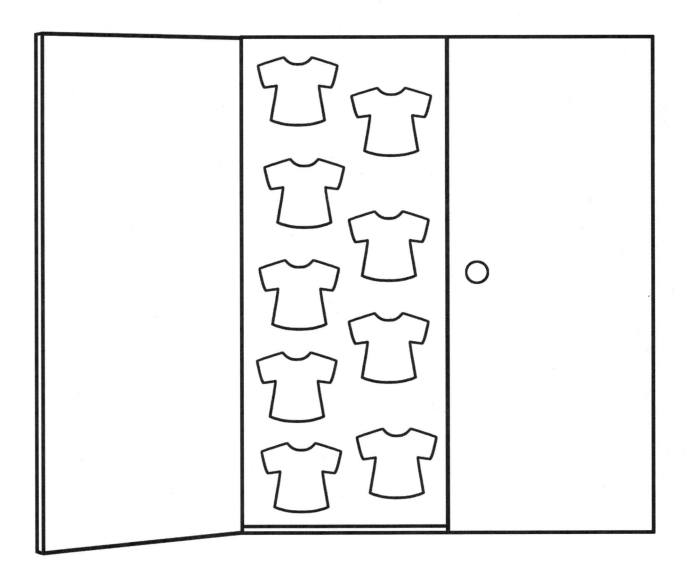

Trace and say. Color the pictures.

The children trace the lines with different colored crayons. Next, the children identify the shadow clothing items. Finally, they color in the clothing items on the right.

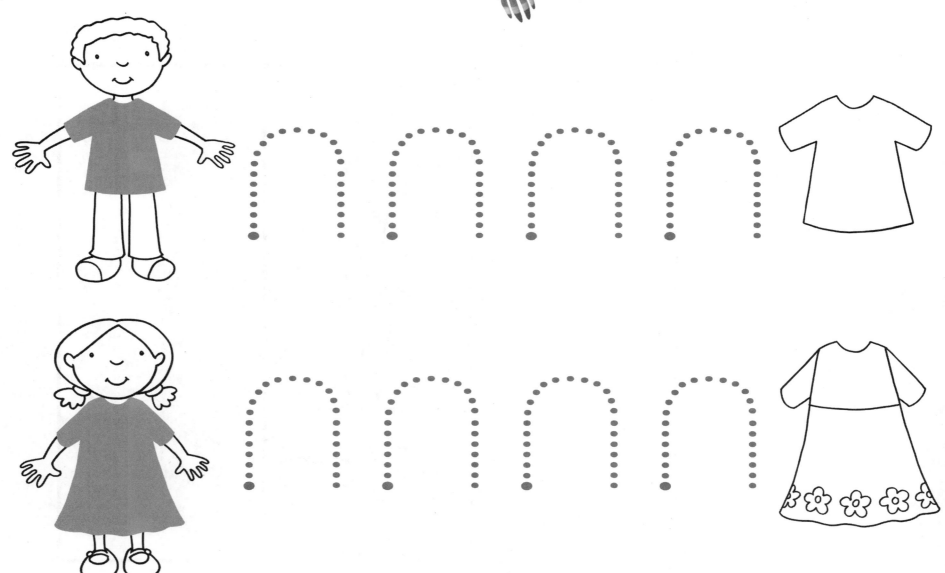

1 **Count and trace. Color the pictures.**

The children count the shoes aloud. Then the children trace the number with their index finger first, and then with different colored crayons several times. Finally, they color in the pictures.

1 **Trace. Listen and color.**

The children trace the lines with different colored crayons. Then the children follow instructions to color in the clothing items; *Show me your blue crayon. Color the T-shirt blue.*

1 **Count and color. Trace the numbers.**

The children count the clothing items aloud. Then they color them in. Finally, the children trace the numbers with different colored crayons.

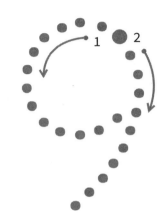

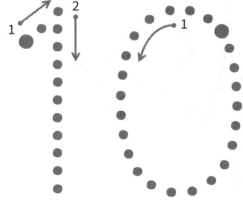

1 **Trace and color.**

The children say /n/ – /n/ – /n/ – *net*. Then they trace the letter and color in the picture freely. Finally, the children color the pictures that start with the letter /n/.

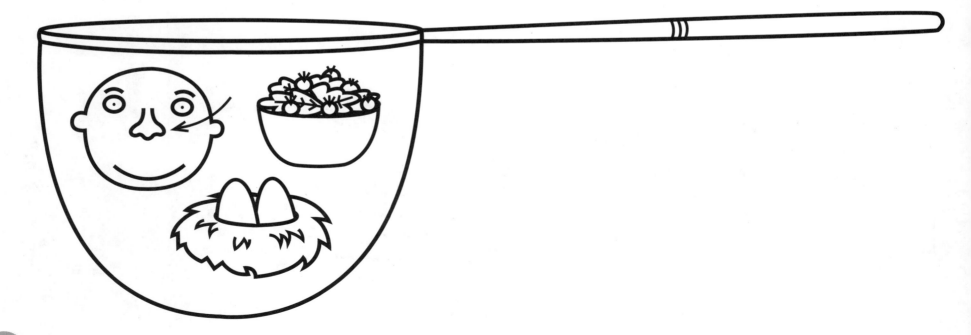

1 **Make a clothes line.**

Fold

Fold

Fold

Fold

Make a clothes line.

Materials:
colored crayons, string, scissors

Preparation:
Cut out string the length of your classroom.
Hang it to make a clothes line inside the
classroom at children's eye level.

Instructions:
The children color in the clothes. Then they
cut out the pieces. Help the children fold
the flaps on the clothing items.
Finally, the children hang their
clothes on the clothes line.

1 **Listen and color. Match the clothes.**

Give the children instructions to color the clothing items in the boxes, *Color the T-shirt blue.* Then the children match the clothing items in the boxes to the boy's clothes.

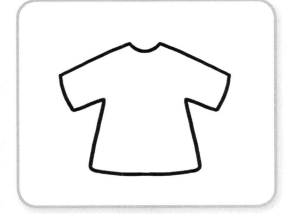

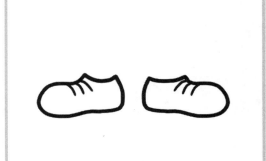

9 My park

The children trace the shapes with different colored crayons. Then the children identify the playground equipment. Finally, the children color in the pictures freely.

1 Trace and color.

   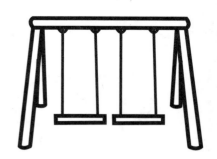

1 Count and trace.

The children count the characters aloud and trace the numbers with different colored crayons. Finally, they color the pictures freely.

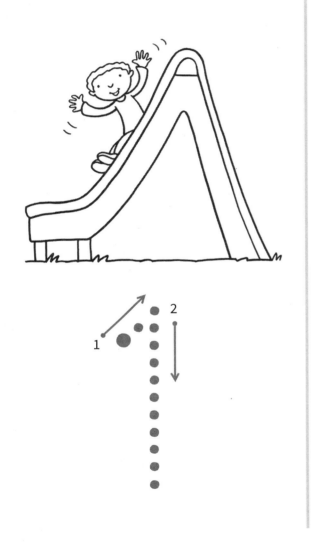

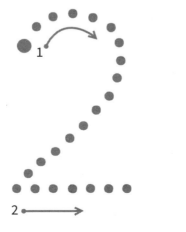

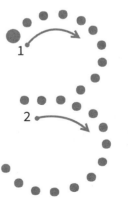

1 **Trace and color.**

The children trace the shapes with different colored crayons. Say sentences and have children identify the pictures; *Point to the boy. Down you go! Point to the girl. Up you go!* Finally, the children color them freely.

1 Count and trace. Color the picture.

The children count the characters in the picture. Then they trace the numbers with different colored crayons. Finally, the children color the pictures freely.

1 **Trace and color.**

The children trace over the shapes with different colored crayons. The children name the playground equipment. Finally, children color in the scene.

n u n u n u n u

o i o i o i o i

1 Count and trace.

The children count each of the shapes aloud. Then they trace the numbers with different colored crayons.

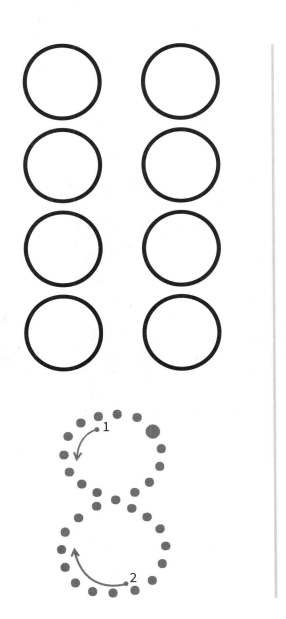

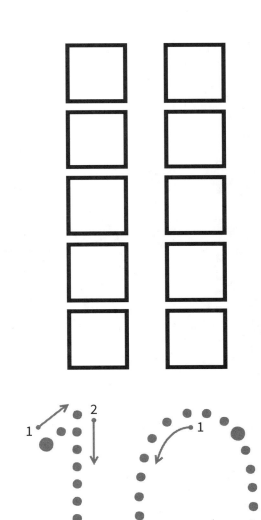

1 **Trace and color.**

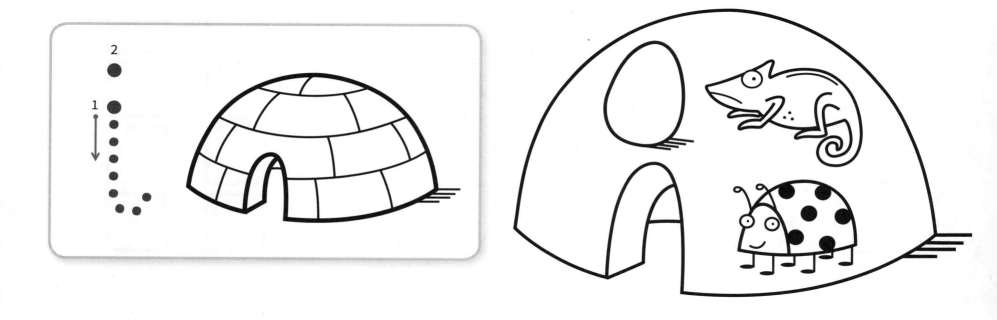

1 Make a park.

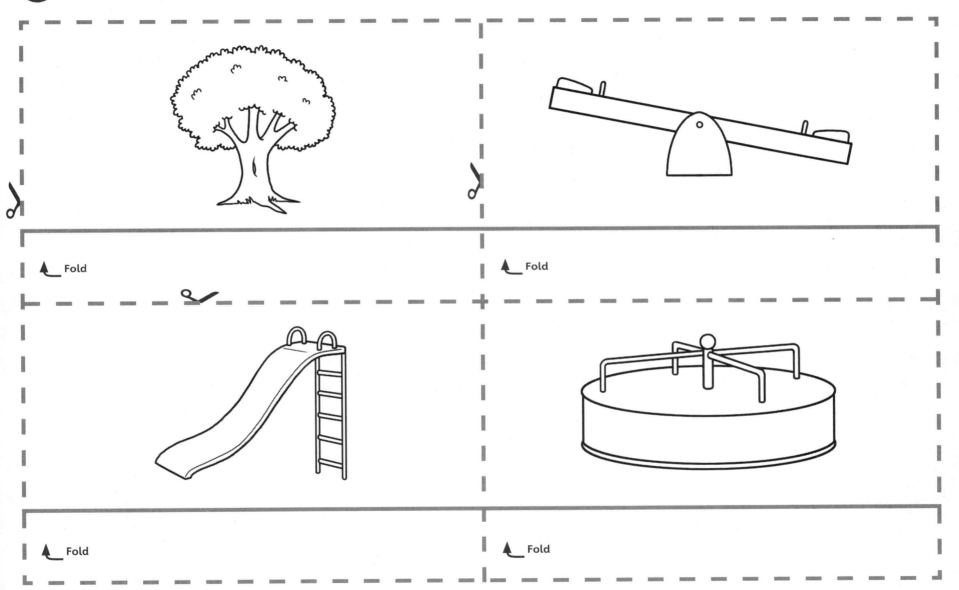

Fold

Fold

Fold

Fold

Make a park.

Materials:
scissors, glue, crayons, shoebox lid, green markers

Instructions:
The children color in the pictures and cut them out. Then they identify the playground equipment and the tree. Next, the children color the shoebox lid green. Show the children how to fold the bottom of each of the pictures to make them stand, and glue them onto the lid.

1 ## Look and match.

The children identify the big and small playground equipment. Then give instructions for children to match the big playground equipment with the small one. Finally, the children color the pictures freely.

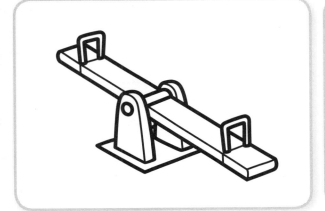

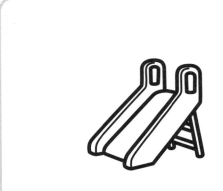

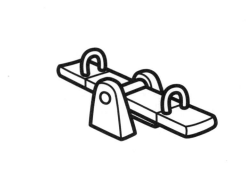

Thanks and acknowledgements

The publishers are grateful to the following contributors:

Blooberry Design: cover design, book design, publishing management and
page make-up
Bill Bolton: cover illustration

The publishers and authors are grateful to the following illustrators:

Bill Bolton 1, 4, 20, 23, 40, 43, 46, 69, 90, (1 and repeats on all pages of Polly);
Louise Gardner 6, 7, 8, 11, 15, 18, 25, 28, 30, 35, 38, 41, 49, 51, 55, 59, 60, 68,
73, 75, 77, 80, 85; Marek Jagucki 31, 43, 53, 58, 63, 67, 71, 81, 83, 95; Sue King
(Plum Pudding) 5, 10, 21, 27, 61, 65, 78, 79, 87, 88, 89, 93; Bernice Lum 9, 12,
13, 16, 17, 19, 22, 26, 29, 32, 33, 36, 37, 39, 42, 45, 48, 50, 52, 56, 57, 62, 66, 70,
72, 76, 82, 86, 92